SUZY BOGGUSS

AMERICAN FOLK SONGBOOK

A companion book to the album

American Folk Songbook
by Suzy Bogguss
© 2011 Loyal Dutchess Books
All Rights Reserved

All songs Public Domain.
Arrangements by Suzy Bogguss
© 2011 Zoe Mahoney Music, BMI
All Rights Reserved
Adapted for the piano by Will Barrow

For more information on the songs please visit:
www.suzybogguss.com

Printed in Canada

CONTENTS

Shady Grove...10

Red River Valley...14

Froggy Went A-Courtin' 18

Shenandoah 23

Sweet Betsy from Pike 26

Wayfaring Stranger 30

Swing Low Sweet Chariot 35

Rock Island Line..38

Wildwood Flower 44

Johnny Has Gone for a Soldier.....................50

Careless Love 55

Git Along Little Dogies 60

All the Pretty Little Horses 66

Erie Canal..73

Banks of the Ohio 78

Ol' Dan Tucker 82

Beautiful Dreamer..87

FOREWORD

Prepare yourself for enchantment!

Folk music is music honoring our common legacy by passing along our most cherished stories, memories, music and legends so that our children and their children's children can enjoy the words and wisdom therein and thus perpetuate our culture.

Because of this we all owe a debt of gratitude to Grammy and C.M.A. Award winner Suzy Bogguss who here presents seventeen beloved musical treasures of our heritage, songs which in some cases predate even our nation's founding.

It warms the cockles of my soul to read and listen to her presentation of so much of the musical fabric of our shared heritage — from the story of an amorous amphibian to tumultuous train rides, mule-powered vessels, our trailblazing westward migration, cowboys herding cattle, the work songs of sailors and the wartime laments of soldiers.

One of the wonderful elements of folk music is that it's meant to be sung by, well, folks, ordinary people, not trained singers, the story is more important than the delivery, it's the song, not the singer. If you should be so moved by this lovely book that you decide to seek out Suzy's vocals of these songs you will hear delightfully unpretentious versions of these classics, beautifully sung, played by A-list Nashville musicians, free of bombastic production and complex arrangements.

Soon, you'll find yourself singing along, taking the journey back, back, back into the days when folk music and songs such as these were a primary means of communicating news and stories of the human condition.

This work is, in a word, delightful!

— John Lomax III

INTRODUCTION

I am often asked when I knew I wanted to be a singer. I used to say that it caught me off guard; that I studied art and the music sort of sneaked up on me. Now that I'm older, it has become evident that I knew I'd be a singer when I was 5 years old.

My family attended church every Sunday a block from our home—four children and my mom (Dad only attended on holidays). We were all involved with the music, and I joined the Angel Choir as soon as I was old enough—5. Etched in my mind is a photograph of my mom and me sitting together in our big soft chair where she taught me to sight-read the alto parts in our hymnal. (Thanks, Mom.) I could soon pick out a harmony to most any song, and that gift made me a standout at Girl Scout camp. (Ha!)

Music has always been my purest joy, my release and the way I appreciate life. When my career became too hectic and threatened to get in the way of that feeling, I pulled back from the "limelight," concentrated on my family and sought out the genuine love I had for singing again. Going back to a more intimate show was all I needed. It came back slowly, performance by performance and sing-along by sing-along.

In the summer of 2008 I toured with the brilliant and engaging Garrison Keillor and his fabulous band. The energy that passed between the audience and Garrison was overwhelming at times, and I cried at more than a few shows. At intermission, after the band and I left the stage, G.K. stayed and led a sing-along while the audience stood and stretched. The response was spectacular! Several thousand people standing and singing together—old songs, hymns, the Beatles, the Everly Brothers. People of all ages, sharing music. Ahhh, pure joy.

So was that the inspiration for this project? Yes, but it was also the realization that I knew those songs because I had been fortunate enough to have music in school. One of my favorite memories is the image of my grade-school music teacher pounding on the piano and leading us all in rousing renditions of folk songs from all around our great country. I was learning, but it was all about fun for me. I feel lucky to have had passionate music teachers who encouraged all of us to participate.

As I started doing research for this collection, I added a few chestnuts into my performances. I heard lovely, touching stories from audience members about learning these songs from parents or grandparents, and lots of "I learned it on my first instrument, the harmonica"—or "the guitar" or "the piano." One friend even said it made her get her guitar out from under her bed. I felt a real drive to make this CD happen.

Then it expanded to "What if there were a book, too?" That way, younger generations could share these slowly fading gems with their families and tell their stories of how they learned a few chords on the guitar or a couple of favorites to play at family gatherings.

The good old fifth-grade songbook was my model, though I couldn't find a copy anywhere. Maybe it's better that way, because my memory of it is kind of nostalgic, the pages indistinct with dreamy pictures and music staffs. I think of how my imagination ran wild with the stories from those songs. I enlisted my husband and writing partner, Doug Crider, to help me put this book together. We had so much fun learning about the history of these enduring songs. It's my hope that I've piqued your interest, too, and that you'll want to share your own stories with family and friends, like in the good old days...heck, these ARE the good old days. Enjoy them!

NOTES

ON THE SHEET MUSIC

My goal in producing this book was to encourage people to participate in folk music—not just to be aware of these wonderful songs, but to actually play and sing them. I wanted to stay true to the spirit of the CD, but I also wanted to make sure that everyone at every skill level was included.

My aim was to make the sheet music comfortable to play and sing. To that end, the songs are often presented here in keys that differ from the recording. Where that's the case they are in the key that I felt best represented the song for all three: piano, guitar and voice.

My friend Will Barrow helped adapt the piano pieces so that they would not be intimidating. Most of the songs are arranged so that the piano part also includes the melody, but some of the folkiest songs were best left to just rhythm and chords (hootenanny!).

Diagrams of the guitar chords are shown with their names above. I use a guitar capo a lot to make a song feel good to play, but also comfortable to sing. When a capo should be used I note it at the beginning of the song, and the chords are shown as they would be played with the capo on. I also included the name of the chord without the capo immediately next to the chord diagram so that piano players can improvise. For instance, on the piano "Old Dan Tucker" plays best in the key of F, but the guitar is more enjoyable to play in the key of D, so the first guitar chord shown is a D with the capo on the third fret.

I hope you'll find this book entertaining and educational, but I especially hope you'll find it fun! Folk songs are meant to be shared by everyone. You can play this—have no fear!

SHADY GROVE

I pretty much cut my teeth as a performer hanging around folkies and bluegrassers. Songs like "Shady Grove" were simple enough for me to chime right in, even at my first jam. In most versions, Shady Grove is a person, but in some circles they sang, "I'm bound for the Shady Grove" as if it were a place. Others sang the rhyme, "Shady Grove my darlin', I'm goin' back to Harlan." I chose to sing about Shady Grove as if she were a little girl I had to leave behind from time to time, as I've had to do with my son when I travel.

The "Harlan" above is Harlan County in southeastern Kentucky. If you're looking for Shady Grove, that's as good a place to start as any.

American folk music comes from all over: cowboy songs from Texas, sea shanties from New England, spirituals from the deep South. But one of the richest veins comes out of the mountains of southern Appalachia, where Tennessee, North Carolina, Virginia and Kentucky crowd together. The area has given us some of the earliest examples of country, bluegrass and old-time music, including the Bristol recording sessions in 1927 that introduced Jimmie Rodgers and the Carter Family— often considered the "Big Bang" of country music.

Why here? Times were (and still can be) hard. The tradition of families playing and singing music together was deep-seated. The coves and hollers made it difficult to travel, so once a song was established in one valley, it stayed there and would evolve independently, separate from how it might be played in the next valley over.

Folk revivalist Jean Ritchie, who grew up near Harlan, is perhaps most closely associated with "Shady Grove." She recalls a story her father told about the first time he heard a fiddle played:

"I just couldn't mortally stand to sit still on that log bench and that tune snakin' around so. No sir, that was one tune that didn't stay in one place no time atall. I was hot and itching all over myself, and I thought to my soul I was going plum crazy. You could hear feet a-stomping all over the house, benches a-screaking, young'uns a-giggling, and nobody a-studying fit for a dog.... The teacher tried to settle us, put us back to our books, but I couldn't even see the print in that speller. I kept seeing that old fiddle bow race around on 'Shady Grove.'"

Shady Grove

Lively and Rhythmic

Traditional

bound   to   go   a – way

Cheeks   are   like   a
Went   to   see   my
Wish   I   had   a

bloom – in'   rose   eyes of a   deep – est   brown
Sha – dy   Grove   (she's) stan–din'   in   the   door
needle   and   thread   fine   as   I   could   sew

she's   the   dar – lin'   of   my   heart   stay   till the sun goes
shoes   and   stock –in's   in   her   had   Little   bare   feet   on
(I'd) sew   my   true love   to   my   side   (and) down the   road   I'd

down
(the) ground
go

bound   to   go   a – way

4. Wish I had a big fine horse
   Corn to feed him on
   Pretty little girl to stay at home
   And feed him when I'm gone

5. There's peaches in the summertime
   And apples in the fall
   If I can't have the girl I want
   I won't have none at all

RED RIVER VALLEY

Whether I'm playing in this country or abroad, I close my shows with this song. It doesn't seem to matter where it originated, everyone loves it, and most know the words. Me, I love a cowboy song. There are some folks who think of me as a yodelin' cowgirl! I don't know if the old-time cowboys used to say, "bid me adieu" (suspiciously northern), but that's my story and I'm sticking to it!

The handsome ranch hand sits atop his pony in the fading light singing this sentimental ballad to his sweetheart who's headed back east. Or the fair Indian maiden of the north sings the song to her beloved departing soldier. Or even (gasp!) the song is sung by gentrified folk around a parlor piano in upstate New York.

Well, of course "Red River Valley" is a cowboy song—countless renditions by crooning cowpokes in grainy western movies have forever established it as such. But it may not always have been so. Each of the scenes above has some claim on "Red River Valley."

The Red River of the western song is the tributary of the Mississippi that forms the border between Oklahoma and Texas. But there is another Red River that flows northward between Minnesota and North Dakota and finally empties into Lake Winnipeg in western Canada—the so-called Red River of the North. Stories tell of the Woolsey expedition of 1870 in which Canadian troops were sent west to put down a local uprising in the Red River Valley. According to these stories, the song was written by an Indian maiden in love with a soldier from the expedition who was being called back to Ontario.

The earliest printed sheet music of the song bears the date 1896 and the title "The Bright Mohawk Valley." The Mohawk is a tributary of the Hudson River in upstate New York. Some evidence suggests the song may have begun here as a parlor ballad.

Wherever it began, the Red River Valley has covered a lot of ground and has been known by many names. In 1929, Texan Jules Verne Allen had the first popular hit with the song under yet another title, which probably best describes how we think of the song today. It was called simply "Cowboy Love Song."

Red River Valley

Moderately

Traditional

From this val-ley they say you are
long time my dar-ling I've
think of the val-ley you're

leav-ing We will miss your bright eyes and sweet smile for they
wait-ed for those sweet words you nev-er would say Now at
leav-ing Oh how lone-some how drear' it will be Do you

4. As you go to your home by the ocean
   May you never forget those sweet hours
   That we spent in the Red River Valley
   And the love we exchanged mid the flowers

FROGGY WENT A-COURTIN'

It's not just a kids' song—folks of all ages love "Froggy Went A-Courtin'." And that makes sense, because this frog's been a-courtin' this mouse for more than 400 years! You might not remember all 171 verses, but if you heard it or sang it like I did as a kid, it's still in there...uh-huh.

Froggy rode up to Miss Mousey's door in a Scottish songbook printed in the year 1611. (But there are mentions of the song, without the music, in publications 60 years before that!) The title of the 1611 version was "The Marriage of the Frogge and the Mouse." The Frogge "would a woing ride, humble dum humble dum, sword and buckler by his side, tweedle tweedle twino." Pretty similar to today's lyrics! A buckler is a small shield, and those went out of fashion in the Middle Ages, but the story of the frog and mouse courtship has changed very little in 400 years.

As for "humble dum" and "tweedle twino," those are what is called a "burden"—a repeated phrase at the end of a line. In current versions we usually sing the phrase "uh-huh, uh-huh" for the burden, but over the years that part of the song has changed—a lot! When Froggy crossed the Atlantic, he settled in the Appalachian and Catskill mountains, and over the centuries the funny, nonsense lyrics of the burden changed in countless ways. In some versions the burden actually became the most important part of the song, and even the title. Songs like "Kitty Alone," "Kemo Kimo" or "King Kong Kitchie Kitchie Ki-Me-O" may not sound very froggy, but they all tell the same amphibious tale.

All the different songs passed lyrics back and forth in so many ways that today it's hard to tell where one stops and another begins. But Froggy and Miss Mousey don't show any signs of stopping—after four centuries they're still planning that wedding. Of course some things do change: In 1611 the wedding supper was "three beans in a pound of butter." These days it's "a fried mosquito and a black-eyed pea." Uh-huh, uh-huh, yum yum!

Froggy Went A-Courtin'

Bouncy (like a frog!)

Traditional

No pedal throughout

(after D.S. sing verses 5, 6, 7)

Frog-gy went a-court-in' and he did ride uh huh —
rode - up - to - Miss Mou-sey's door uh huh He
took - Miss - Mou - sey on his knee uh huh He
Not with- out my Un - cle Rat's con -sent uh huh —

Frog-gy went a-court-in' and he did ride uh huh —
rode - up - to - Miss Mou-sey's door uh huh He
took - Miss - Mou - sey on his knee uh huh He
Not with- out my Un - cle Rat's con sent uh huh —

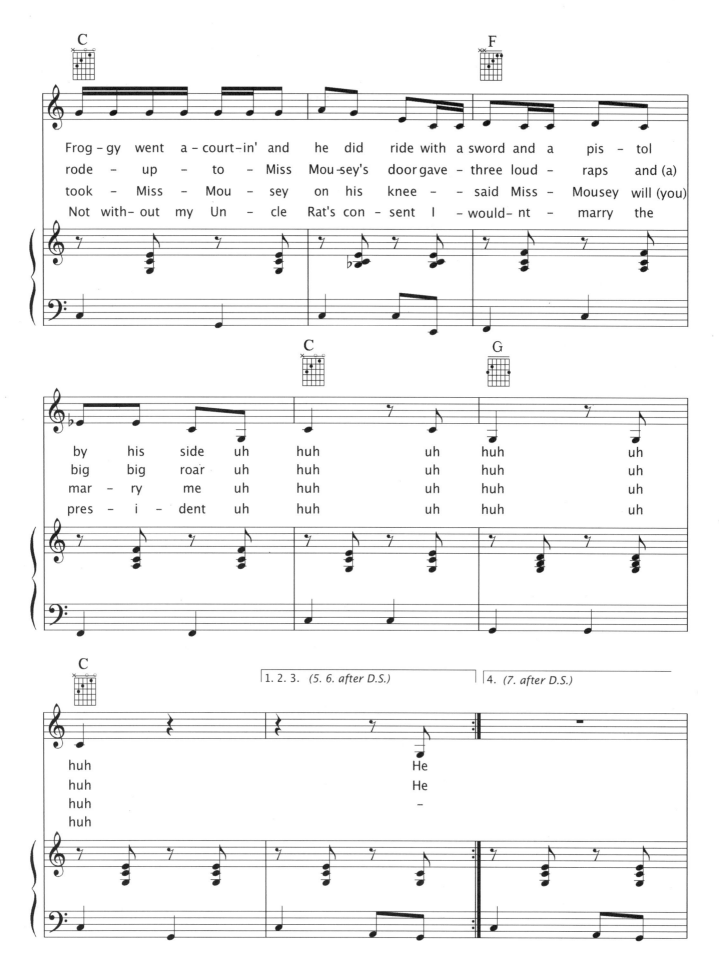

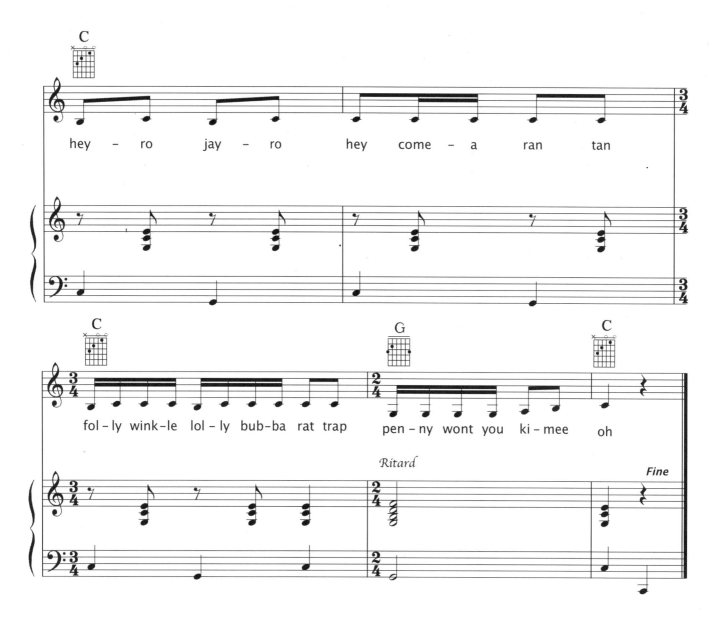

5. Where shall the wedding supper be, uh huh
   Where shall the wedding supper be, uh huh
   Where shall the wedding supper be
   Way down yonder in a hollow tree, uh huh, uh huh, uh huh

6. What should the wedding supper be, uh huh
   What should the wedding supper be uh huh
   What should the wedding supper be
   Fried mosquito and a black-eyed pea, uh huh, uh huh, uh huh

7. A little piece of cornbread layin' on a shelf, uh huh,
   A little piece of cornbread layin' on a shelf, uh huh,
   A little piece of cornbread layin' on a shelf
   If you want any more, you gotta sing it yourself, uh huh, uh huh, uh-huh

SHENANDOAH

As a daughter of a river valley myself —the mighty Mississippi—I easily identify with Shenandoah's wistful longing for home. I chose to sing the more sentimental universal lyrics, but the other verses are beautiful as well. I've included some of them here.

Here's the best song ever written about a picturesque valley...or a mighty river...or an Indian chief. Huh? Well, this much we know: It's really a sea shanty!

As with many folk songs, it's impossible to know where "Shenandoah" was composed, or even exactly what it's about. One interpretation of the story tells of a homesick pioneer's nostalgia for the Shenandoah River Valley in Virginia and his love for a young woman who is its daughter. In another version, a Missouri River trader spends seven years courting the daughter of an Indian chief, Shenandoah. Yet another is told from the Indian maiden's standpoint: She is stolen from her tribe, the Senados, and is longing for her home on the Shenandoah River.

Regardless of where it originated, the song eventually caught on with the flatboatmen of the Missouri and Mississippi rivers and found its way south to the sea. Along with coffee and cotton, sailors carried folk songs down the Mississippi, through the Gulf of Mexico and the Caribbean, to the populous cities of the East Coast and back again. As the crew members changed, so did the words to the songs.

Sailors used rhythmic tunes called sea shanties to help coordinate their chores. For instance, a rigorous call-and-response song might be used for the harder "heave-ho" type of work, like hoisting the sails. "Shenandoah" is an example of slower-paced, more nostalgic shanties. It's easy to imagine the voices of the sailors singing the sweeping, wave-like melody as they prepared to put down anchor in the home port or cast off for someplace far away.

Though the lyrics changed from sailor to sailor, the pattern of repetition was always the same. The first and third lines may alter the story, but the second and fourth lines, "Away you rollin' river" and "Away, I'm bound away," return each time.

So it doesn't matter if Shenandoah is a river or a valley or an Indian chief, the emotion expressed by this beautiful reflective melody is the same—a longing for home, even though I'm bound away.

Shenandoah

Expressively

Traditional

Alternate Lyrics:

Oh, Shenandoah, I love your daughter
Away, you rolling river
It was for her I'd cross the water
Away, I'm bound away, cross the wide Missouri

Now the Missouri is a mighty river
Away, you rollin' river
Indians camp along her border
Away, I'm bound away, cross the wide Missouri

Well a white man loved an Indian maiden
Away, you rolling river
With notions his canoe was laden
Away, I'm bound away, cross the wide Missouri

For seven long years I courted Sally
Away, you rolling river
Seven more years I longed to have her
Away, I'm bound away, cross the wide Missouri

SWEET BETSY FROM PIKE

With high spirits and expectations, Betsy and Ike set out to make the most of an opportunity. I just love 'em! Betsy is a fireball, and Ike is so real I can almost hear his voice. They do such a great job of holding each other up during the long trek until a jealousy gets in the middle of them. Back in school I got the biggest kick out of the last line, "Goodbye you ol' lummox, I'm glad you backed out." People don't use "lummox" enough anymore.

"Old Put" set out from Missouri in 1849, bound for the gold fields of California. He poked around in the mud for a while looking for gold, but spent most of his time in the music halls and gambling houses around Placerville. He did find a nugget once, but folks say it wasn't from mining—he fell and hit his head on it outside a saloon. He took to singing his own made-up songs to the boys in the tent camps, where he was paid in gold dust.

That may sound like a tale from a folk song, but it's the true story of the man who wrote one of the best-known songs of the California Gold Rush. John A. Stone, who performed as "Old Put," organized his own band of traveling musicians called the Sierra Nevada Rangers. They entertained miners with songs Stone wrote, mostly to the tunes of older folk songs. Old Put finally "struck gold" when he collected his verses in several editions of pocket songbooks, which together sold more than 25,000 copies. His second collection, Put's Golden Songster, was published in 1858 and contained "Sweet Betsy From Pike," which, according to Stone's notes, should be sung to the tune of the popular English song "Vilikins and His Dinah."

Gold was discovered at Sutter's Mill in California in 1848, and some 6,000 adventurers came searching for fortune that year. There may have been as many as 90,000 in 1849. (The term "forty-niner" was a reference to miners who arrived in that year.) Some came by sea, but most came overland following the California Trail from the Missouri River. The hardships they endured on the 2,000-mile trek were many, including cholera, Indian attacks, freezing, drowning, starving, and being run over by wagons. After such a difficult journey, it's understandable that Betsy, Ike and Old Put himself might have wanted to kick up their heels. In the preface to Put's Golden Songster, John Stone wrote: "I have endeavored to portray, as graphically as possible, life in California, at a time when the restraints of society had to some extent become released...."

Sweet Betsy From Pike

John A. Stone

Lively

4. They soon reached the desert where Betsy gave out
   And down in the sand she lay rolling about
   While Ike, half distracted, looked on with surprise
   Saying, "Betsy, get up you'll get sand in your eyes"

5. The terrible desert was burning and bare
   And Isaac he drank from the death lurkin' there
   Dear old Pike County, I'll come back to you"
   Says Betsy, "You'll go by yourself if you do"

6. They suddenly stopped on a very high hill
   With wonder looked down on old Placerville
   Ike sighed when he said, and he cast his eyes down
   "Sweet Betsy my darling, we've got to Hangtown"

7. They swam the wild rivers and climbed the tall peaks
   And camped on the prairies for weeks upon weeks
   Starvation and cholera, hard work and slaughter
   They reached California, spite hell and high water

8. Long Ike and Sweet Betsy attended a dance
   Ike wore a pair of his Pike County pants
   Sweet Betsy was dressed up in ribbons and rings
   Says Ike, "You're an angel, but where are your wings?"

9. 'Twas out on the prairie one bright starry night
   They broke out the whiskey and Betsy got tight
   She sang and she howled and she danced o'er the plain
   And showed her bare legs to the whole wagon train

10. A miner said, "Betsy, will you dance with me?"
    "I will, you old hoss, if you don't make too free
    But don't dance me hard, do you want to know why?
    Doggone ye, I'm chock full of strong alkali"

11. Long Ike and Sweet Betsy got married, of course
    But Ike, getting jealous, obtained a divorce
    While Betsy, well satisfied, said with a shout
    "Goodbye, you ol' lummox, I'm glad you backed out"

WAYFARING STRANGER

This was one of the first songs I learned to play on the guitar. The chords were fairly simple but the melody takes you from a minor key to a very uplifting major chorus. Pretty impressive to all of my non-musical camping pals back then. It was in all of my books; guitar, grade school music and our Presbyterian hymnal. Sometimes they labeled it a folk song, sometimes a spiritual, and sometimes a hymn. I like that.

Folk songs are passed along by memory, one generation teaching them to the next. And that's fine if you just want a tune to plunk out on your banjo with some friends. But if you're going to sing a song in church, and you want everyone to sing it together, you have to find a way to write it down.

Early pioneers had a tough time getting to church. They didn't live in cities with actual church buildings. Most settlements didn't have clergy, either, so in the early 1800s preachers would travel around and hold camp meetings. People would come from great distances to attend, and the meetings would last for several days, so travelers would camp in tents on the meeting grounds.

The camp meetings were raucous, festive occasions, a chance for folks to take a break from the difficult routine of pioneer living. Singing hymns together was an important part of the gatherings. As meetings became larger and more popular, the lyrics to the hymns began to be collected in books called songsters. "Wayfaring Stranger" is probably even older than the camp meetings, but the first time the words show up in print was in one of these songsters.

As the country grew and religious services became more formalized, the words were combined with music notation in books we would recognize today as hymnals. Not everyone could read music, though, so congregations came up with inventive ways of writing songs down. One of the more interesting that survives to this day is a style called shape-note singing, in which notes on the page are given shapes to represent what pitch should be sung. Shape-note singing relies heavily on a book called The Sacred Harp that has been in continuous publication since 1844. (The sacred harp is the human voice.)

Today you can still find "Wayfaring Stranger" in The Sacred Harp, as well as in standard hymnals, folk and bluegrass songbooks, and in formal arrangements for classical ensembles and choirs. Obviously many ways have been found to write it down—but if you like, you can still plunk it out on your banjo.

Wayfaring Stranger

Shuffle feel

Traditional

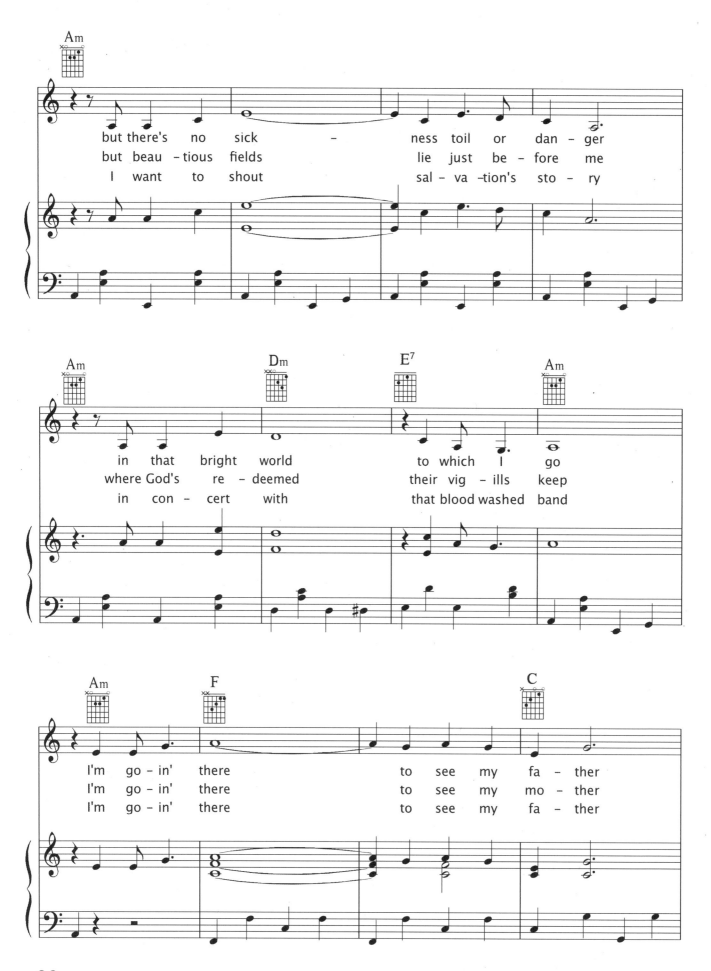

SWING LOW
SWEET CHARIOT

Seems as if I've always known this song. It's another call-and-response tune, and when these simple words meet this powerful melody it really packs a wallop! Oppression, redemption and retribution.... When I sing "Swing Low Sweet Chariot," I feel heavy and light at the same time!

In 1871, when Alexander Reid attended one of the first performances of the Fisk Jubilee Singers, he was asked how he liked the material. "Very well," he replied, "but I have heard better."

He wasn't bragging. In 1849, Reverend Reid served as missionary to the Choctaw Nation at a school in Oklahoma. In those days the Choctaw had adopted the Southern custom of owning slaves. "Uncle" Wallace Willis and his wife "Aunt" Minerva were slaves who occasionally helped Reid with chores. Uncle Wallace composed songs that he and Minerva would perform for the students. These songs, including "Swing Low Sweet Chariot," "Steal Away to Jesus" and "Roll, Jordan Roll," are some of today's best known spirituals.

Well known, but perhaps not well understood. The lyrics of spirituals often functioned on several levels. Certainly they were sincere expressions of faith. But on another level, they were a way for slaves to offer up strength and hope to one another, to communicate through the lyrics while working the fields. The Master became Pharaoh, and escape into freedom became crossing the river Jordan. At times the songs may have even included coded messages for escape plans.

The Fisk Jubilee Singers were the first group to begin performing African-American spirituals in public. Fisk University in Nashville was founded in 1866 as the first university to offer liberal arts degrees to students of color, and the Jubilee Singers began as a way to raise money for the college. The director of the chorus, George L. White, would routinely ask audiences to contribute songs they might know. At one of these shows, Reverend Alexander Reid presented himself to White and offered to teach the Uncle Wallace songs.

"It flashed into my mind," Reid would later write, "that I could furnish him with some pieces—genuine plantation songs...and thus help on the good cause of education among Freedmen.... I sometimes feel as if I must have been inspired for that special occasion. I don't know one note from another, and never could master the courage to start a tune in meeting. Yet...I stood up before Professor White and his trained "Jubilees"...and sang my six songs over and over again until I had anchored [them] firmly deep down in their hearts."

Swing Low Sweet Chariot

Expressively

"Uncle" Wallace Willis

looked o - ver Jor-dan and what did I see... Com-in' for to car-ry me
some times - up - and some - times down... Com-in' for to car-ry me
I get -there - be-fore - you do... Com-in' for to car-ry me
you get -there - be-fore - I do... Com-in' for to car-ry me

home A band of an - gels com-in' af - ter me...
home But still my soul feels heav-en - ly - bound...
home I'll cut a hole and pull - you - through...
home Tell all my friends - I'm - com - in' too...

(last time)
D.S. al Fine

Com - in' for to car - ry me home Swing
Com - in' for to car - ry me home Swing
Com - in' for to car - ry me home Swing
Com - in' for to car - ry me home Swing

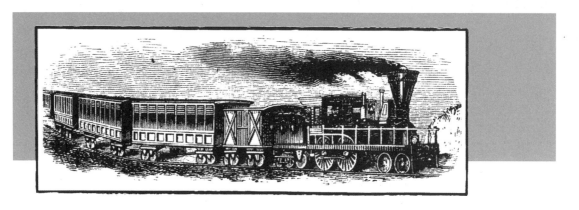

ROCK ISLAND LINE

In the small town of Aledo, Illinois, where I grew up, the train passed through about a block from my house. My grandfather was a telegrapher and part-time depot master a couple of towns up, and we kids could ride the "Dolly" up to visit. I've always loved trains, and to this day when I hear a whistle blow in the distance I think it's my Gramps sayin' hello. The renowned railroad ran east and west about 20 miles from Aledo. I can still close my eyes and see the rusty brown cars with Rock Island line printed in white on the sides.

Two men came together in 1934 to collect folk songs. One was a respected folklorist and college professor from Texas. The other was an uneducated black man from Louisiana who had spent much of his adult life in prison.

John A. Lomax was the preeminent collector of American folk music. Over the course of his life he recorded and preserved more than 10,000 songs. Working for the Library of Congress, Lomax traveled around the United States with a phonograph, recording folk songs in hotel rooms, churches and prisons. In July 1934 he traveled to the Louisiana State Penitentiary to record convicted murderer Huddie Ledbetter—or as he was called by his fellow inmates, Leadbelly.

Just a month after that recording session, which produced the folk classics "Goodnight Irene" and "Midnight Special," Huddie was given early release from prison for good behavior. Needing employment to fulfill the conditions of his parole, he begged Lomax for a job. Leadbelly became the expedition's driver and recording assistant.

One of their first stops was a prison in Gould, Arkansas. To break the ice, Lomax had Huddie perform. The folklorist would later write: "When the twanging of his guitar strings rang out, supporting his rich booming voice, silence fell in the rows of cells suddenly and completely." The pair recorded a group of convicts singing "Rock Island Line," a call-and-response work song. Leadbelly logged it away in his memory. Years later he would record it in his own style, and it became the often-copied, definitive version.

For three months, John and Huddie traveled the backroads of the South together. In 1935 Lomax headed to New York to promote his book American Ballads and Folk Songs, and he brought Huddie with him. The press loved the story of the "singing convict," and Leadbelly became a sensation. For a few months Leadbelly and Lomax traveled together as celebrities, but they eventually had a falling out over money and parted ways. They never collaborated again, but the last concert Leadbelly performed before his death in 1949 was at the University of Texas, and was a tribute to his mentor, John A. Lomax.

Rock Island Line

Train Rhythm

Traditional

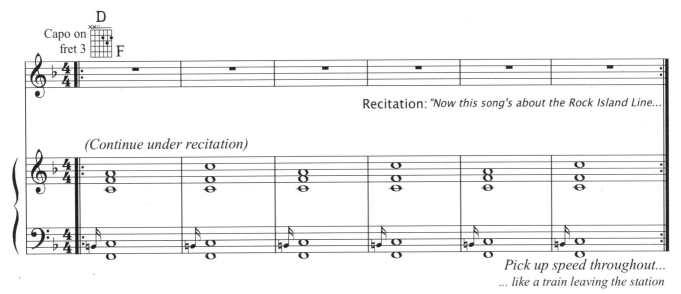

Recitation: *"Now this song's about the Rock Island Line...*

(Continue under recitation)

Pick up speed throughout...
... like a train leaving the station

...I got all pig iron"

Now The

No Pedal Throughout

Rock Is-land line   is a migh-ty good road... The Rock Is-land line   is the

road to ride The Rock Is-land Line.... is a migh-ty good road if you

want to ride it got-ta ride it like you find it get your tic-ket at the sta-tion on the

Rock Is-land line (last time) To Coda ⊕ ...a little faster (I) may be right and I

may be wrong but you're gon-na miss me when I'm gone

40

Ha - le lu - ia I'm... saved from sin... the good Lord's com - ing for to

see me a - gain

D.S. al Coda CODA *...a little faster*

A   B   C   W

X   Y   Z   The cat's in the cup - board but he   don't see

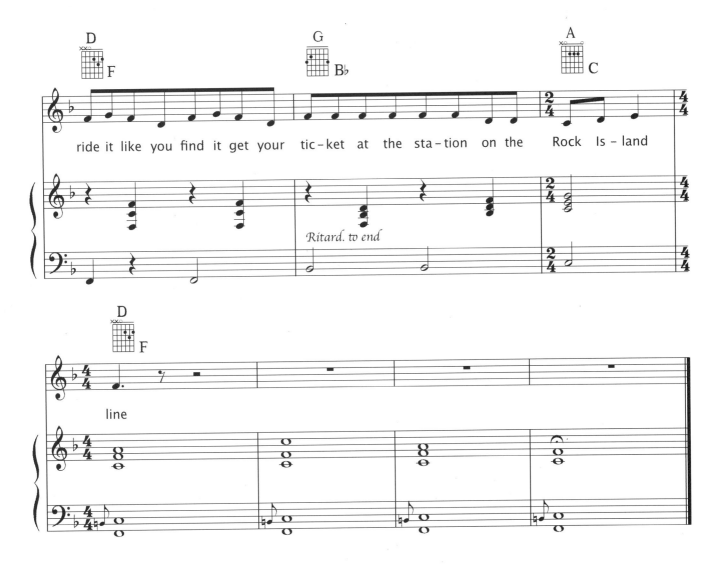

Recitation:

Now this here's the story of the Rock Island Line. Now the Rock Island Line runs down into New Orleans, and just outside of New Orleans is a big toll gate. And all of the trains that go through the toll gate, well, they gotta pay the man some money. Now of course if you just have certain things on board, then you don't have to pay the man nothin'. Well, just now we see a train makin' it's way down the line. And when she comes up to the toll gate, the driver, he shouts down to the man and he says:

(Sung)
"I got pigs, I got horses, I got cows, I got sheep,
I got all livestock, I got all livestock, I got alllll livestock"

And the man says, "Well you alright then just get on through. You don't have to pay me nothin'!" And the train goes through. And when he goes through the toll gate the train gets up a little bit of steam.....and a little bit of speed. And when the driver thinks he's safely on the other side, he shouts back down the line to the man. He says:

(Sung)
"I fooled you, I fooled you,
I got pig iron, I got pig iron, I got alllll pig iron"

WILDWOOD FLOWER

As a singer, I often move words around to suit my phrasing or the melody more comfortably. I even change words sometimes, by choice or accident. When I started to research "Wildwood Flower" for my recording session and found the elegant lyrics that Maud Irving wrote, I was all the more excited about singing this long-loved tune. I found that the girl in the story was no sad sack, but a tenacious woman with a specific goal in mind. She was going to flaunt her newfound confidence and put her past behind her. Atta girl!

In his day, Joseph Philbrick Webster was a fairly well known songwriter—one of his hymns, "In the Sweet By and By" is still sung today. Maud Irving was a poet about whom very little is known. Her enduring claim to history is a poem entitled "I'll Twine 'Mid the Ringlets," which Webster set to music in 1860. The sweet little parlor song was popular for a time but eventually fell out of fashion. It might have faded away completely had it not been for later events.

Remember the old game Telephone? A person whispers a message to a second person, who passes it to a third and so forth, until it reaches the last person, who says the message out loud. At that point the message has often changed so much that it has a totally different meaning. That's sort of how folk songs work.

More than half a century after "I'll Twine 'Mid the Ringlets" was written, young Maybelle Addington learned the song at the knee of her grandmother. As a young woman, Maybelle, her cousin Sara Carter and Sara's husband A.P. began playing music together as the Carter Family. In 1928, when recording was in its infancy, they recorded several songs for the Victor label. The session, a cornerstone of country and folk music, included the song Maybelle's grandmother had taught her, which she knew as "Wildwood Flower."

Because the Carter Family had learned the song "by ear," some words were replaced with others that sounded similar. "I'll twine 'mid the ringlets of my raven black hair," became "I'll twine with my mingles and waving black hair." Sometimes the changes gave the song a completely new meaning: Irving's proud heroine declares, "I'll live yet to see him regret the dark hour, when he won, then neglected, the frail wildwood flower," while the Carters' narrator suffers when she cries, "I long to see him and regret the dark hour, he's gone and neglected this pale wildwood flower."

The lyrics of "Wildwood Flower" continue to be reinterpreted today. It seems Maud Irving and J.P. Webster started a game of Telephone in 1860 that we're still playing!

Wildwood Flower

With a lively rhythm

Joseph P. Webster
Maude Irving

Vocal

I   will

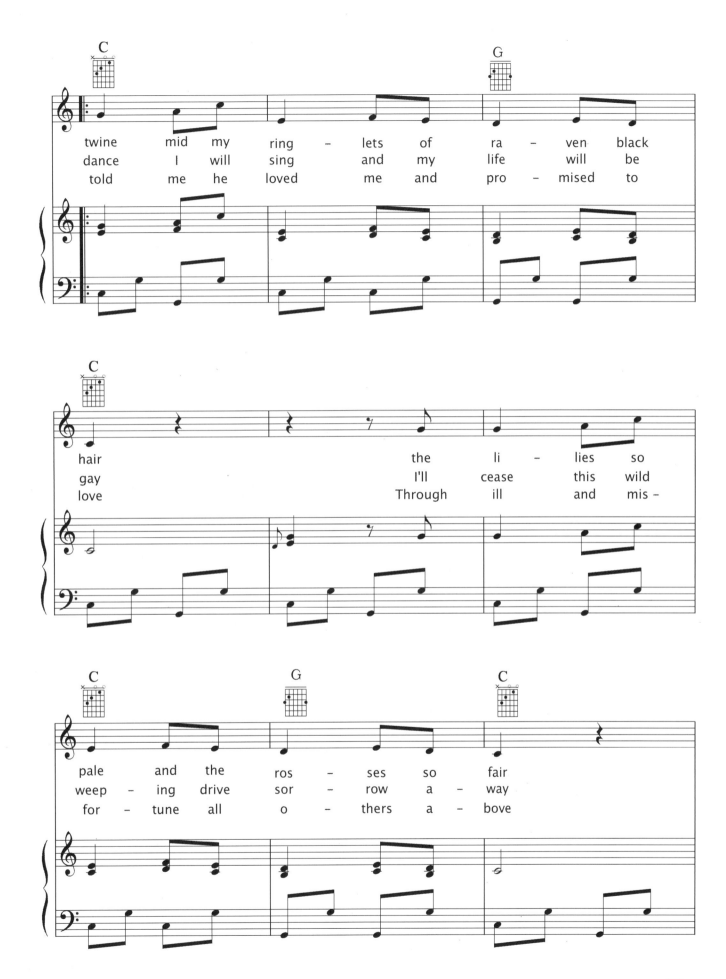

twine mid my ring – lets of ra – ven black
dance I will sing and my life will be
told me he loved me and pro – mised to

hair the li – lies so
gay I'll cease this wild
love Through ill and mis –

pale and the ros – ses so fair
weep – ing drive sor – row a – way
for – tune all o – thers a – bove

4. He taught me to love him, he called me his flower
   That blossomed for him all the brighter each hour
   But I woke from my dreaming, my idol was clay
   My visions of love have all faded away

5. I'll think of him never, I'll be wildly gay
   I'll charm every heart, and the crowd I will sway
   And I'll live yet to see him regret the dark hour
   He won, then neglected, the frail Wildwood Flower

JOHNNY HAS GONE FOR A SOLDIER

When I was singing this song for the album I felt like I was channeling the girl from the song. A profound sadness came over me, and I get the same feeling each time I sing it. Our girl here is inconsolable. Nothing means much to her now that her true love has left for war. She wallows in self-pity, but knows that anyone who sacrifices this way will understand. She sold her most prized possessions to do what she could to take care of her man. Now all she can do is wait and worry. It seems she won't even be herself, just wandering through the streets until he is back and they are married. I have never been in such a predicament, and still it chokes me up to sing her story.

At the Battle of Monmouth, the men of George Washington's Continental Army were hot. The temperature topped 100 degrees on that day in late June of 1778, and amid the gunfire came the sound of men crying out for women to fetch them a drink of water: "Molly, pitcher!" According to an eyewitness, one of these women attended a cannon, and in the process, "...a cannon shot from the enemy passed directly between her legs without doing any other damage than carrying away all the lower part of her petticoat...looking at it with apparent unconcern, she observed that it was lucky it did not pass a little higher...."

The story became known as the legend of Molly Pitcher, and whether this particular tale actually happened, women did follow their husbands into battle during the American Revolutionary War. They were called camp followers, and in addition to their performing the necessary jobs of cooking, sewing and nursing the wounded, their practice of following the troops was a way to keep families together during this extremely difficult time. Camp followers were officially sanctioned by the military, but they were required to be married to a soldier; sweethearts were left behind.

"Johnny Has Gone for a Soldier" is the tale of one such sweetheart. The song is based on an older Irish song, "Shule Agra" or "Siúil a Rúin." It evolved and was adapted by Americans and became one of the more popular songs of the Revolution. The heroine of the song laments that her Johnny has left her to go and fight and lists the sacrifices she is willing to make to ensure his safe return.

It's possible there may have been another, more famous camp follower that day in Monmouth, New Jersey. Martha Washington frequently traveled with her husband throughout the entire eight years of the War for Independence.

Johnny Has Gone For A Soldier

Moderately slow

Traditional

54

CARELESS LOVE

This was such a simple little folk song in my first piano book. I remember it having repetitive lines that were none too happy (love gone wrong and all that), but later when I found these lyrics...my, how a few verses with very personal words can take a song from a sad story to a sultry blues. That's an amazing thing about songs like these—an individual's trials can determine how dramatic the song will be. I didn't sing the folksy words from my childhood but instead chose a version of the lyrics that brings out regret and consequences. I wanted to sing the blues.

"Careless Love" is a traditional song in the style that today is known as the blues. When William Christopher Handy was asked in a 1929 interview whether the blues had any relation to folk music, he replied, "Yes, they are folk music." And W. C. Handy, the "Father of the Blues," would have known.

Legend has it that the blues were born on a dark night in 1903 at a lonely train station in Tutwiler, Mississippi. Handy, a classically trained bandleader, had fallen asleep on a bench while waiting for his train. He awoke to the sounds of a tattered man singing in a strange, mournful tone while sliding a knife across the strings of his guitar. "It was the weirdest music I had ever heard," Handy recalled. This may have been the exact moment when the blues first met a musician capable of writing it down.

So what defines the blues? Handy might have said it was a shuffling, uneven rhythm combined with a melody that emphasized the lowered third, fifth and seventh notes. He might also have noted the lyrical repetition—the first line repeated two or three times and a longer final line. Or he might have simply said it was the moody, despondent message that somehow made you feel good inside.

W.C. Handy would go on to write countless blues songs and have a lasting influence on American music. One of his compositions, "Loveless Love," was based directly on "Careless Love." Incorporating existing folk songs into more contemporary styles was an accepted tradition. In that 1929 interview Handy stated: "Each one of my blues is based on some old Negro song of the South, some folk song that I heard from my mammy when I was a child...some old song that is a part of the memories of my childhood and of my race. I can tell you the exact song I used as a basis for any one of my blues. Yes, the blues that are genuine are really folk songs."

Careless Love

Bluesy shuffle feel

Traditional

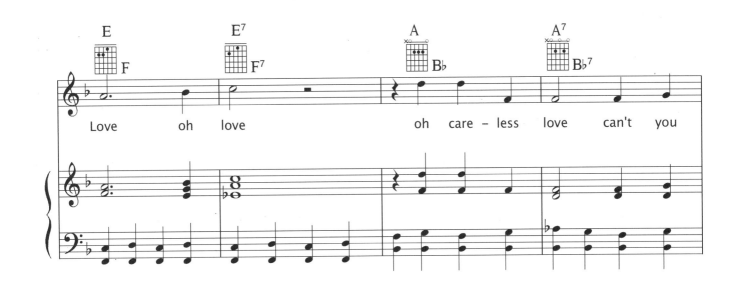

Love   oh   love   oh   care – less   love   can't   you

(last time)
To Coda

see   what   care – less   love   has   done

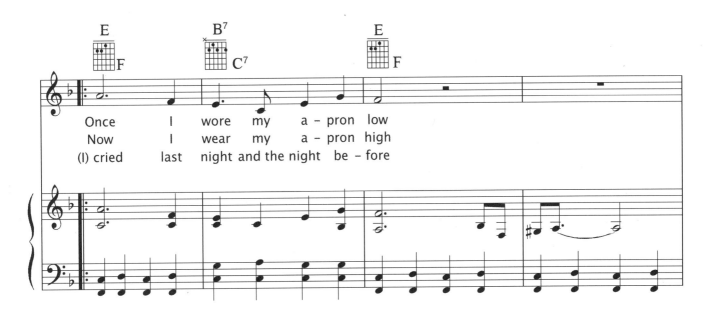

Once   I   wore   my   a – pron   low
Now   I   wear   my   a – pron   high
(I) cried   last   night and the night   be – fore

GIT ALONG LITTLE DOGIES

When I was 12, I was lucky enough to hang out with Roy Rogers and Dale Evans. My grandparents lived on their same block in Apple Valley, California. When I visited, I could scarcely believe they considered the legendary Western stars friends. I guess that's when my love for cowboy music and yodeling took root. I added the yodel to "Git" because I simply couldn't resist.

"You wanna call me that, smile." Gary Cooper speaks that famous line to the mustachioed villain in a scene from the movie *The Virginian*, based on Owen Wister's classic novel of the same title. The book was an immediate success when it was published in 1902 and is often credited with creating the iconic image of the American cowboy.

Wister was an educated aristocrat from Philadelphia, but he loved the American West of the 1880s. He made many trips west, hunting, fishing and researching his books, so he knew a real cowboy when he saw (or heard) one. His journals, discovered in 1952, contain the earliest complete record of the song "Git Along, Little Dogies."

After the Civil War, the new process of meat-packing had made beef more valuable than ever. Texas had cattle but no railroads, so for 20 years cowboys would drive cattle north to a railhead where they could be shipped to the northern packing plants. The song "Git Along, Little Dogies" tells the historically accurate story of a roundup to take dogies from Texas to Wyoming.

"Dogies" were motherless calves that tended to fall behind and had to be nudged along, but the whole herd might be called dogies when they needed encouragement. Cowboys did indeed "mark 'em and brand 'em and bob off their tails," and they really did sing to the cattle to calm them. But "some boys go up the long trail for pleasure"—that's where the song got it wrong. The work was difficult, so cowboys were mostly very young. Some were Civil War veterans. About a quarter were African-Americans, around 15 percent were Mexican, and a sizable number were Native Americans.

By the time Owen Wister created *The Virginian*, railroad expansion had all but ended the great cattle drives. Cowboys were still around, though, singing the praises of a life on the open range. In his journal, Wister wrote: "I have come upon a unique song...and I transcribe it faithfully. Only a cowboy could have produced such an effusion. It has the earmark of entire genuineness."

Git Along Little Dogies

Cowboy Waltz

Traditional

Whee - dee - dee - dee - dee - yay oh - dee - oh - da
(Yodel)

lay - ee - dee

As I was a rid - ing one
It's ear - ly in (the) spring when we
Your mo - ther was raised – –

morn - ing for plea sure I spied a young cow - boy a - rid - in' a -
round up the do gies we mark -'em and brand 'em and bob off their
way down in Tex - as where Jim - son — weed and the chol - - las

long His hat was thowed back and his spurs was a - jing - lin' and
tails — Round up the hor - ses load up the chuck wa - gon and
grow — We'll fill you up on that prick - ly pear cac - tus un -

as he rode by he was sing - ing this song Whoop - ee
throw them little do - gies out on the north trail
till you are rea - dy for I - - da - ho

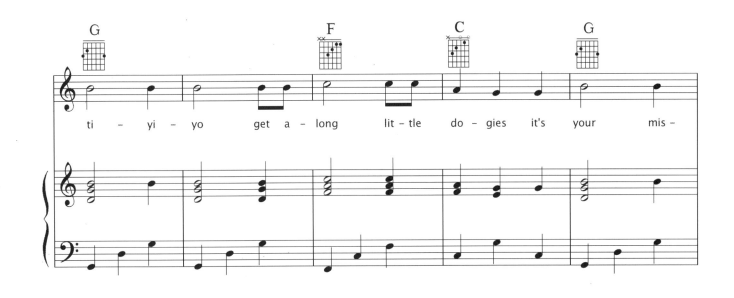

ti – yi – yo   get a – long   lit – tle   do – gies   it's   your   mis –

for – tune   and   none   of   my   own   Whoop – ee   ti – yi   yo   get a –

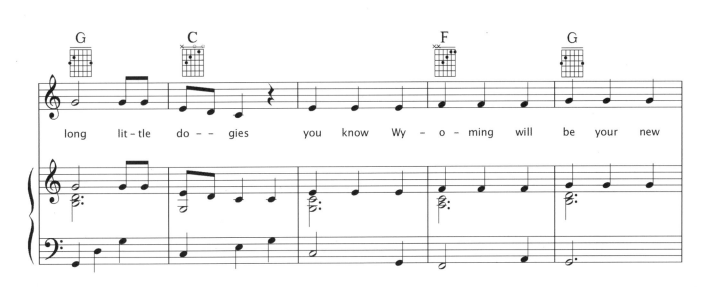

long   lit – tle   do – – gies   you   know   Wy – o – ming   will   be   your   new

dee - oh - da - lo - hoo   ah - dee - oh   lay - ee - oh   da   lay - ee-

dee

ritard.

4. Some boys go up the long trail for pleasure
   But that's where they get it most awfully wrong
   You'll never know the trouble they give us
   As we go a–drivin' them dogies along

ALL THE PRETTY LITTLE HORSES

When my son Ben was small he didn't like songs with ominous-sounding minor chords. If the church organist started a song like that, Ben would huddle up to me as if he instinctively knew it was something scary. I wonder if we can get that feeling only after our imagination has developed enough to know that there are things to fear?

This beautiful American lullaby, with its dark but soothing melody and comforting images of dappled horses, butterflies and cake, has hushed many a crying child off to dreamland. But in its earliest form, it may have caused a few nightmares as well.

The song has its roots in the American South, where slave mothers were often separated from their own infants and called upon to tend to the master's children instead. Listen closely—there are actually two babies in the song: the Master's child, who will have the all the pretty little horses, and the "poor little lamby" in the second verse who cries for his mammy.

The lamby in the meadow was a way for the singer to privately refer to her own newborn, who certainly needed his mother. But instead of the familiar lyric "bees and butterflies flutter 'round his eyes," the earliest known versions of the song alarmingly describe "birds and butterflies pickin' at his eyes."

The song was a form of quiet protest, but there may have been another reason for including such a chilling scene. Many fairy tales and nursery rhymes contain scary images—the knife-wielding farmer's wife in "Three Blind Mice," for example, or the munchkin-munching witch in "Hansel and Gretel." Lullabies can be frightening, too: Remember the poor baby in the treetop? "When the bough breaks the cradle will fall, and down will come baby, cradle and all." Ouch! Several reasons have been suggested for why we find these kinds of images in traditional children's songs. They may have been a way to prepare the child for troubles later in life, or to contrast how safe they are in mother's arms. An older explanation is that the words were used as a kind of charm to scare off evil spirits.

But if evil spirits and demanding masters aren't a problem, the fluttering butterflies and lovely melody should help a little one drift off to sleep quite nicely.

All The Pretty Little Horses

Delicately

Traditional

coach and six-a-lit-tle hor — ses Blacks and
poor little thing's a-cry-in' Mam — my

bays dap-ples and grays all the pret-ty lit-tle

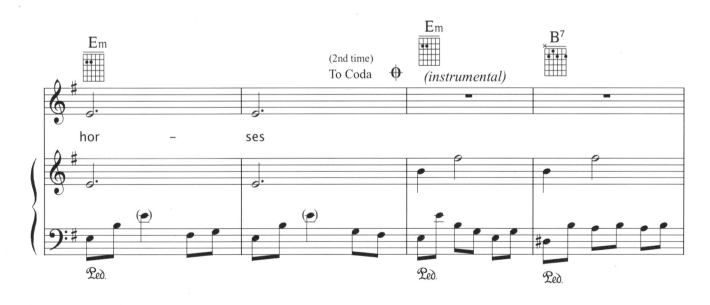

hor — ses

(2nd time)
To Coda ⊕ (instrumental)

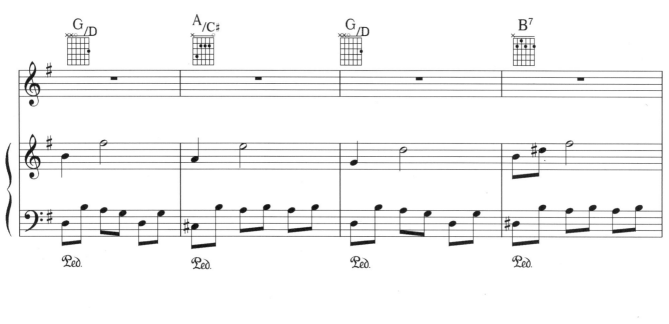

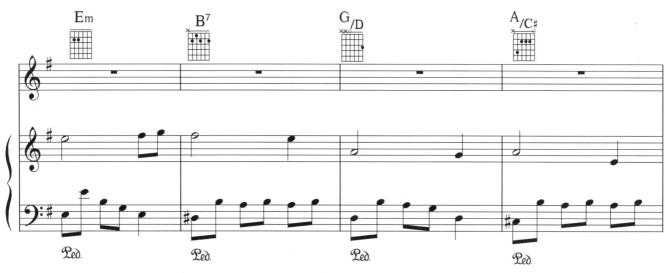

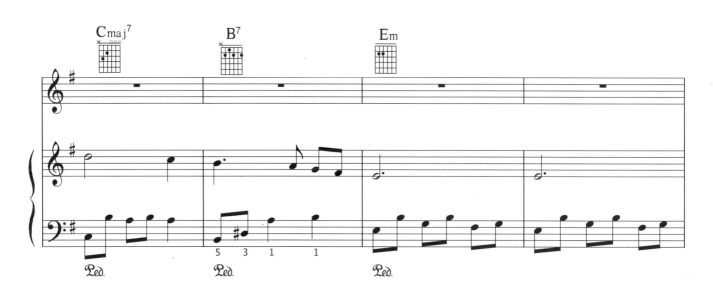

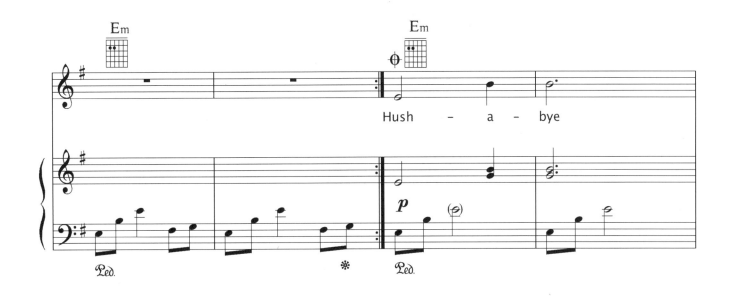

you shall have all the pret - ty lt - tle hor — ses

ERIE CANAL

When I told people about the folk song CD, "Erie Canal" was on the tip of everybody's tongue. When my class sang it in fifth grade, we practically shouted it! It's such a memorial of the time when the canal was first used and folks would break up the long trips with lusty singing (or fights!). Though there is a note of sadness in the eminent change ahead, I just envision cheerful people who had bettered their lives boldly singing about the good old days when they or their parents worked on the canal, celebrating that they had been a part of something truly great.

"Low bridge!" If you'd ever worked on the Erie Canal—and by the end of the 19th century so many had—you knew what that meant. So it became a joke about how to spot pretenders among New York's "upper crust": Yell the phrase in a roomful of society folk and 19 out of 20 would duck their heads!

The idea of connecting the Atlantic Ocean to the Great Lakes with a waterway had been discussed since the early 1700s. A canal across New York to Lake Erie would allow goods to travel easily and cheaply from Europe to what was then considered the American West.

Work was finally begun in 1817, and when the Erie Canal was finished in 1825 it stretched 363 miles from Albany to Buffalo through a series of more than 80 locks. During its heyday, barges navigating the canal were pulled by mules walking along the shore, but by the turn of the 20th century the mules had been replaced by steam and diesel power. So it was with a sense of nostalgia that Thomas S. Allen wrote his famous song about the canal in 1905. It tells the story of a mule driver who works for 15 years on the Erie Canal with his pal, a mule named Sal. In later versions, the word "years" was replaced by "miles," signifying the distance a mule could travel before needing to rest.

The title of the song was originally "Low Bridge, Everybody Down." The story goes that the state of New York promised to build bridges over the canal for farmers' cattle to get from one pasture to the next—but they never promised the bridges would be high! That's why experienced canal travelers reflexively ducked whenever they heard, "Low bridge!" And that's why Thomas Allen was so sure "you'll always know your neighbor, you'll always know your pal if you've ever navigated on the Erie Canal."

Erie Canal

Thomas S. Allen

75

ev-er nav-i-ga-ted on the Er - ie Ca - nal

BANKS OF THE OHIO

Growing up, I used to play this one over and over from my sister's piano book. It was hypnotic and kind of creepy. The song is written from the murderer's standpoint, recounting the details of the event in a sort of stunned, melancholy haze. Somehow it always seemed like I could feel the ghost of the girl in there too.

Folk music has a dark side. Dig up those pretty wildflowers and you might find a shallow grave. Look deep enough into that rolling river and you may see a body pinned under a rock. The murder ballad goes back as far as murder... and that's a long way back.

Why would we harmonize about violent death? Well, many murder ballads are tales of remorse and retribution, where the villain eventually gets his rightful comeuppance. Often there's a moral to be learned as the scoundrel admonishes the listener not to "do what I done." It may also be that the murder ballad is a cautionary tale, reminding us that a darkness lurks even in the hearts of those we know best.

A traditional ballad, as historians like to define it, is a verse form that became popular in the Middle Ages that usually told a narrative story—sometimes invented, but often true. In those days verses were printed on large single sheets of paper called broadsides and hawked by traveling salesmen who would actually sing the songs for their clientele (sort of a really old-school version of TV news anchormen). It's easy to understand why ballads about real events were popular: Nothing grabs your attention like a song detailing the brutal murder of your neighbor from the next village over.

American murder ballads took hold in the cramped hollows and close harmonies of Appalachia. As far as is known, "Banks of the Ohio" is not based on any historical event, but it certainly feels real enough. The evildoer regrets his terrible deed in the end, but that doesn't soften this tale of a gruesome stabbing and drowning. It could have been worse, though: In another old murder ballad, "Down in the Willow Garden," the victim is stabbed, drowned, and poisoned!

Banks of the Ohio

Moderately

Traditional

No pedal throughout

I asked my love to take a
if she'd mar – ry
knife a –gainst her

walk to take a walk just a lit – tle ways and as we
me – and my wife for – ev – er be she on – ly
breast and told her she was –going to rest she cried oh

4. I took her by her lily–white hand
   And led her down the bank of sand
   And there I threw her in to drown
   And watched her as she floated down

5. And going home 'tween twelve and one
   I cried, "Dear Lord, what have I done?"
   I've killed the only girl I love
   Because she would not marry me

OLD DAN TUCKER

I'm in love with this irresistible character! It brings out my bossy side to sing this song and scold Old Dan for comin' in too late for supper. I even get a bit of pleasure imagining how his face falls when he gets the news that he's gonna go hungry. Mean, huh?

This cantankerous old character from the antebellum South was brought to life by a young man from the North. Dan Emmett, Tucker's creator, was a serious musician, yet he performed for most of his career with burnt cork rubbed over his face. He was a strong supporter of the Union during the Civil War, and ironically, the composer of the song "Dixie."

Writing a folk song may have been a bit like making a quilt: a piece of tune from here, a scrap of lyric from there. Historians may disagree about whether Emmett fashioned "Old Dan Tucker" from whole cloth, but without a doubt his performances with the Virginia Minstrels accounted for the song's great popularity.

Dan Emmett was born in 1815 in Mount Vernon, Ohio. At an early age he taught himself to play the fiddle and began writing songs. At 17 he enlisted in the army, but after being discharged for being underage, he joined the circus. There he learned the banjo and first began to perform in blackface, the popular style of the day in which white performers covered their faces and hands with burnt cork and mocked the language and mannerisms of slaves.

In 1843 Emmett teamed with three other blackface performers to form the Virginia Minstrels. Their performance in New York City, singing Emmett's "Old Dan Tucker," is generally considered the first of what would come to be known as a minstrel show, those rollicking revues of songs and jokes about life on the plantation.

In addition to "Old Dan Tucker," Emmett published more than 30 popular songs including "The Blue Tail Fly" and that other famous song he wrote in 1859. One day after the surrender of General Robert E. Lee, Abraham Lincoln addressed a White House crowd: "I thought 'Dixie' one of the best tunes I ever heard. I had heard that our adversaries over the way had attempted to appropriate it. I insisted yesterday that we had fairly captured it."

Old Dan Tucker

Dan Emmett

you're too late to get your sup - per

4. Ol' Dan Tucker came to town
   Ridin' a billy goat leadin' a hound
   Hound barked, the billy goat jumped
   Throwed Dan Tucker up side of a stump

5. Ol' Dan Tucker was a fine old man
   Washed his face in a fryin' pan
   Combed his hair with a wagon wheel
   Died with a toothache in his heel

BEAUTIFUL DREAMER

I simply could not imagine recording a folk record without a Stephen Foster song! When it comes to American music, he is quite simply a wellspring, a founding father. In the 1800s, as immigrants from other countries created the fabric of our culture, Foster wove together melodies and rhythms from those countries to create a treasure trove of brilliant, uniquely American songs that inspired generations of musicians and songwriters. I interpreted this gem as a lullaby, a tender thank-you to a beautiful dreamer. I love the writing, and the writer, and I hope to inspire you to look further into his legacy.

According to the original sheet music published in 1864, "Beautiful Dreamer" was "the last song ever written by Stephen C. Foster." But that was certainly not the case. This beautiful song by America's most famous songwriter had been gathering dust on his publisher's shelf for at least two years prior to his death.

At the age of 21 Stephen Foster wrote "Oh Susanna," which quickly became a huge sheet-music hit and the unofficial anthem of the California Gold Rush. After that early success, he quit his job as an accountant to write songs full-time (an idea completely unheard of at the time). Foster was extraordinarily prolific, composing classics like "Camptown Races," "Old Folks at Home (Swanee River)," "My Old Kentucky Home" and "Jeannie With the Light Brown Hair." He became famous, his songs were in great demand, and it seemed his career choice was working out.

But it was tough to make a living. Foster discovered publishers selling thousands of copies of "Oh Susanna" without his permission. (He is said to have made only $100 on the song.) In the late 1850s his health was failing, due in part to bouts with alcoholism. He moved his family to New York in 1860, but a year later his wife and daughter left him alone in the city.

These are the sad circumstances under which Stephen Foster wrote "Beautiful Dreamer," one of his most cherished melodies. His publishers prepared the song to be engraved in 1862 but didn't release it. In 1864, ill and alone in his Bowery rooming house, Foster fell and hit his head. He died three days later with 38 cents and the scrap of a lyric in his pocket. In a rush to capitalize on the tragedy, Foster's publishers scoured their files, discovered his lost masterpiece and issued sheet music with the inscription: "The last song ever written by Stephen C. Foster, composed but a few days previous to his death."

Beautiful Dreamer

Smoothly

Stephen C. Foster

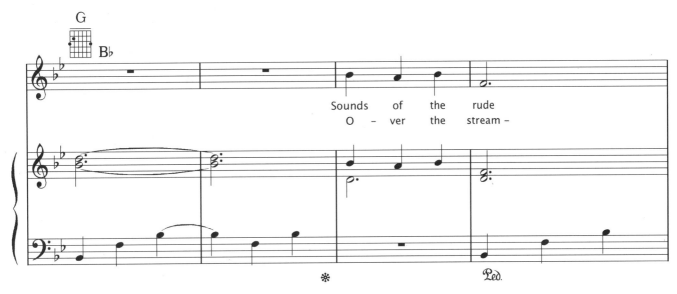

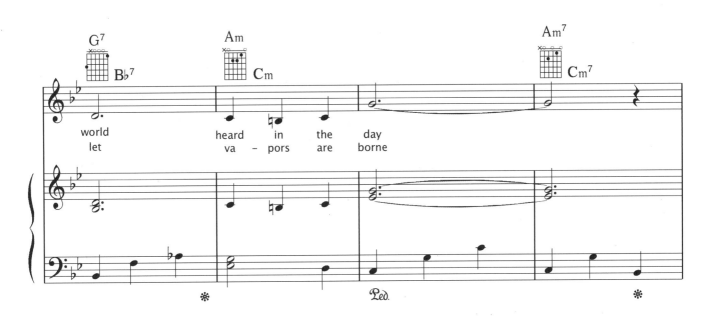

SUZY BOGGUSS

Suzy Bogguss grew up in the small Midwestern town of Aledo, Illinois; close to her family, near the Mississippi River, and surrounded by cornfields. Throughout the '90s Suzy could be heard on country radio with a string of hits, including "Letting Go," "Drive South" and "Hey Cinderella," that bridged the genres of country music and folk music. She has recorded 15 critically acclaimed solo albums and an album of duets with Chet Atkins. Her numerous awards include the 2005 GRAMMY for Best Traditional Folk Album for her contribution to *Beautiful Dreamer: The Songs of Stephen Foster*. Suzy continues to tour and record. She makes her home outside Nashville, Tennessee, with her husband, co-writer Doug Crider, their son Ben, and two small dogs.

Text: Suzy Bogguss with Doug Crider
Edited by: Deb Barnes
Design: Doug Crider
Layout: Annette Krammer
Photography: Amy Dickerson

For more information on the songs please visit:
www.suzybogguss.com

QUOTES

Jean Ritchie
Singing Family of the Cumberlands
The University Press of Kentucky (1988)

John A. Stone
Put's Golden Songster
Appleton & Co. (1858)

Rev. Alexander Reid to Bro. Edwards
Presbyterian (1890)

J. A. Lomax and A. Lomax
Negro Folk Songs as Sung by Lead Belly
Macmillan (1936)

Joseph Plumb Martin
A Narrative of a Revolutionary Soldier:
Some of the Adventures, Dangers and Sufferings of Joseph Plumb Martin
Signet, New York (2001)

Dorothy Scarborough
The "Blues" as Folk-Songs
Journal of the Folklore Society of Texas (1916)

Owen Wister
Owen Wister Out West: His Journals and Letters
University of Chicago Press (1965)

Carl Sandburg
Abraham Lincoln: The Prairie Years and the War Years
Sterling Publishing Company, Inc. (2007)